电子科技系列科普绘本

Serial Pop Science Picture Books on Electronic Sci-tech

你知道与不知道的卫星通信

HOW MUCH DO YOU KNOW ABOUT SATELLITE COMMUNICATION?

(中英对照版)

(Chinese-English Version)

赵 轲 主编 Written by: Ke Zhao

赵 轲 龙 梅 郝聪婷 翻译 Translated by: Ke Zhao Mei Long Congting Hao

电子科技大学出版社

University of Electronic Science and Technology of China Press

·成都·

图书在版编目（CIP）数据
你知道与不知道的卫星通信：汉英对照 / 赵轲主编.
成都：成都电子科大出版社，2024. 12. -- ISBN 978-7-5770-1483-8
Ⅰ. TN927-49
中国国家版本馆 CIP 数据核字第 2025R3X142 号

你知道与不知道的卫星通信（中英对照版）
NI ZHIDAO YU BUZHIDAO DE WEIXING TONGXIN（ZHONG-YING DUIZHAO BAN）
赵轲　主编

策划编辑　谢忠明　黄杨杨
责任编辑　蒋　伊
责任校对　段晓静
责任印制　段晓静

出版发行　电子科技大学出版社
　　　　　成都市一环路东一段 159 号电子信息产业大厦九楼　邮编 610051
主　　页　www.uestcp.com.cn
服务电话　028-83203399
邮购电话　028-83201495

印　　刷　成都久之印刷有限公司
成品尺寸　250 mm×250 mm
印　　张　2
字　　数　46 千字
版　　次　2024 年 12 月第 1 版
印　　次　2024 年 12 月第 1 次印刷
书　　号　ISBN 978-7-5770-1483-8
定　　价　36.00 元

创作团队 CREATION TEAM

顾问 CONSULTANT

陈德利

Deli Chen

儿童顾问 CHILDREN CONSULTANT

陈昕悦

Xinyue Chen

作者 WRITER

赵 轲

Ke Zhao

创作人员 OTHER CREATORS

叶桂兰	郝聪婷	王念慈
Guilan Ye	Congting Hao	Nianci Wang

设计制作 DESIGNER

李媛媛	汤伟东
Yuanyuan Li	Weidong Tang

AR 开发 AR DEVELOPER

苏州和云观博数字科技有限公司

Suzhou AR-Museum Digital Technology Co. , Ltd.

AR 读本这样用
How to Use the AR Books?

1 用手机或平板扫描上方二维码，下载“云观博”APP。

Scan the QR code with your smart phones or pads, and download the "AR-Museum" app.

2 选择“社教”中的“电子科技博物馆 AR 读本”，点击“AR”功能。

Select "the Electronic Science and Technology Museum AR Books" in "Social Education" Section, click the "AR".

3 扫描部分页面中的“ ”（小眼睛图标）。

Scan the icon " " on some pages.

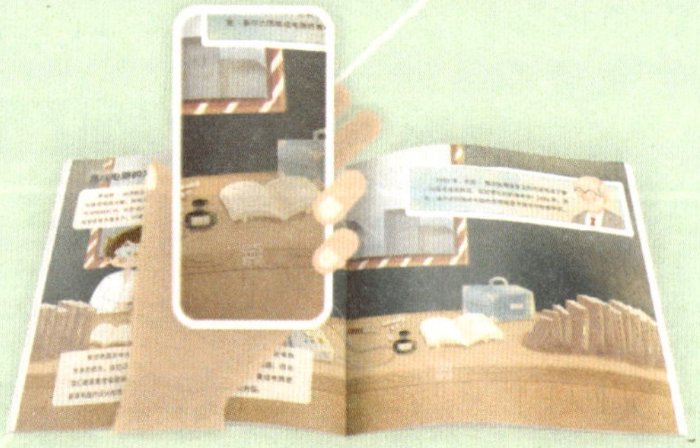

4 看图片、听语音、玩转 3D，还有精彩视频，让你全方位了解这件了不起的发明。

Find more about the amazing invention with pictures, audios and 3D videos.

人物简介
Introduction of Characters

姓名：约翰 · 罗宾森 · 皮尔斯
身份：美国工程师和作家。他对通信卫星的开发起到了重要作用，被称为“卫星通信之父”

Name: John Robinson Pierce
Identity: American engineer, writer, important for the development of communication satellites, "Father of Satellite Communication"

姓名：小科
身份：6 岁的小男孩
性格：充满好奇，喜欢探索和提问，喜欢电子科技产品

Name: Kyle
Identity: Six-year-old boy
Character: Curious, like to explore and ask questions, fond of electronic products

仰望星空
STARGAZING

周末，小科和家人一起来到山上的露营点看星星。夜深了，其他人看完星星都睡了，只有小科兴奋得睡不着。他用手机拍下了美丽的星空，想要将此时此刻的美景分享给朋友。但山上的信号不太好，手机里的照片怎么也发送不出去，小科苦恼极了。这个时候，一位自称是约翰 · 皮尔斯的中年人出现在他身边。

On a weekend, Kyle and his family come to a campsite on the mountains to admire the stars. It is late at night and everyone else is asleep, but Kyle is too excited to sleep. He takes pictures of the beautiful starry sky with his mobile phone, and wants to share them with his friends. But the mobile signal on the mountains is not good, and he fails to send out the pictures. Kyle is frustrated. At this moment, a middle-aged man appears, and calls himself John Pierce.

想把照片发出去吗?
利用卫星通信就可以了。
Want to send out the pictures?
You can use satellite communication.
卫星通信? 什么是
卫星通信啊?
Satellite communication?
What is that?

集成电路的发明
INVENTION OF IC

小科眨眨眼睛，发现自己来到了电子科技博物馆，馆内陈列着许许多多与卫星通信有关的展品。约翰·皮尔斯在这里为小科揭开了卫星通信的秘密。

Kyle blinks, and then finds himself in the Electronic Science and Technology Museum. There are many exhibits related to satellite communication. John Pierce reveals the secrets of satellite communication for Kyle here.

我们常用的无线通信是利用地面移动通信网络，通过多个基站来完成信息的接收和转发，这种方式的通信范围受限于基站信号的覆盖范围。卫星通信则是利用人造地球卫星来接收、转发带有信息的无线电波。卫星通信的通信范围很大，可以实现全球覆盖；可靠性高，在面对自然灾害或陆地通信中断时，卫星通信可以提供可靠的备份通信手段；还可以同时向好几个地点发送信息或接收信息，实现多址通信。

The wireless communication we commonly use relies on mobile communication networks on the ground, and receives and forwards information through multiple base stations. Its communication range is limited by the signal coverage of the base station. However, satellite communication uses artificial earth satellites to receive and forward radio waves with information. Its coverage is global and highly reliable. It can provide a dependable backup communication means in natural disasters or during terrestrial communication disruptions. It can send information to or receive it from multiple locations at the same time, making multi-address communication possible.

卫星通信
Satellite Communication

地面移动通信网络
Mobile Communication Networks on the Ground

想一想　Think

小朋友，你知道卫星通信和我们常用的无线通信有什么区别吗？

Do you know the difference between satellite communication and the wireless communication we commonly use?

世界卫星通信发展简史

BRIEF HISTORY OF WORLD SATELLITE COMMUNICATION

1945 年，28 岁的英国科幻小说家阿瑟 ·C. 克拉克在论文中首次畅想了卫星在通信中的应用。

In 1945, Arthur C. Clarke, a 28-year-old British science fiction writer, first envisioned the application of satellites in communication in his essay.

1960 年，卫星通信进入实验阶段，美国发射世界上第一颗无源（被动）通信卫星“回声一号”（ECHO-1），这颗卫星的成功发射实现了电话、电视的转播。

In 1960, the satellite communication entered the experimental phase. The United States launched the world's first passive communication satellite, ECHO-1, which realized the transmission of telephone and television.

1957 年，苏联用洲际弹道导弹发射了人类历史上第一颗卫星。

In 1957, the Soviet Union launched the first satellite in human history by an intercontinental ballistic missile.

20 世纪 90 年代，移动卫星通信和宽带卫星通信被广泛应用。

In the 1990s, mobile satellite communication and broadband satellite communication were widely used.

1964 年，“辛科姆 3 号”（Syncom-3）成功发射，成为第一颗与地球自转同步的人造卫星。美国和日本利用该卫星第一次实现奥运会的实况转播。

In 1964, Syncom-3, the first satellite synchronized with the earth's rotation, was launched. The United States and Japan used this satellite for the first live broadcasting of the Olympic Games.

20 世纪 80 年代，甚小口径卫星终端站（Very Small Aperture Terminal，VSAT）问世并得到广泛应用，一些国家开始将其应用于共用通信网。

In the 1980s, the Very Small Aperture Terminal (VSAT) was invented and widely used. Some countries began to apply it to shared communication networks.

中国卫星通信发展简史

BRIEF HISTORY OF SATELLITE COMMUNICATION IN CHINA

中国的卫星通信起步较晚，但是现在却发展得很好。

Satellite communication in China started late, but is now well developed.

1970 年，中国自主研制的首颗人造卫星“东方红一号”成功发射，中国成为世界上第五个独立研制和发射人造地球卫星的国家。

In 1970, China's first self-developed satellite, DFH-1 was successfully launched. China became the fifth country in the world to independently develop and launch an artificial earth satellite.

1972 年，时任美国总统理查德·尼克松访华。中国租用了美国的卫星设备进行电视转播和新闻报道，这是中国第一次使用卫星通信。

In 1972, US then-President Richard Nixon visited China. China rented US-made satellite equipment for TV broadcasting and news coverage of the visit. This was China's first use of satellite communication.

1984 年，“东方红二号”成功发射，中国正式开始使用自己的卫星进行通信。

In 1984, DFH-2 was launched. China officially began to use its own satellites for communication.

1986 年，中国第一颗实用通信卫星发射成功，标志着卫星通信由试验阶段进入实用阶段。

In 1986, China's first operational communication satellite was launched. This marks the transition of satellite communication from the experimental phase to the operational phase.

20 世纪 90 年代，中国的卫星发展逐步加速，开始成立企业化运作的运营公司，并承接外国商务。

In the 1990s, China's satellite development gradually speeded up. Operational companies were founded and they began to undertake foreign businesses.

21 世纪，中国进入了卫星通信的黄金时期，并在 2021 年实现覆盖全球的卫星通信能力。

In the 21st century, China enters the golden age of satellite communication. In 2021, it achieved global satellite communication coverage.

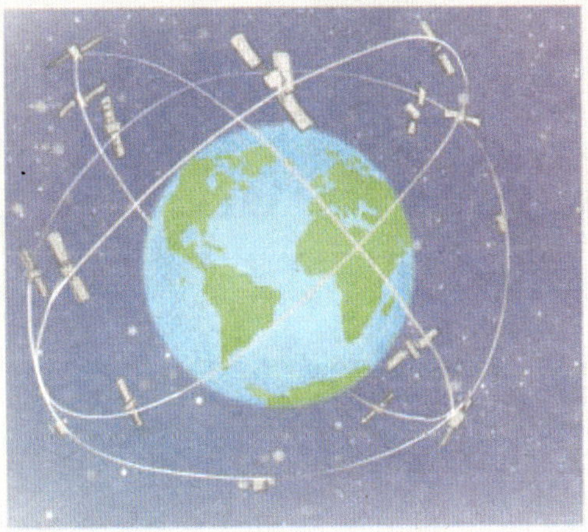

卫星通信的应用

APPLICATION OF SATELLITE COMMUNICATION

卫星通信技术作为一种先进的信息传输手段，不仅促进了全球通信的快速发展，也为多个行业提供了重要的技术支持。

卫星通信的应用非常广泛，例如电话、广播电视、天气预报、导航定位等。其中，提供导航定位服务的导航系统非常重要，它让我们的生活变得更加精彩和便捷。

Satellite communication technology is an advanced means of information transmission. It promotes the rapid development of global communication, and provides important technological support for many industries.

The application of satellite communication is extensive, such as telephone, radio and television, weather forecasting, navigation and positioning. The navigation system makes our life more exciting and convenient, and is very important.

最低 -6 ℃　最高 0 ℃
Lowest: -6° C　Highest: 0° C

全球四大卫星导航系统

WORLD'S FOUR MAJOR SATELLITE NAVIGATION SYSTEMS

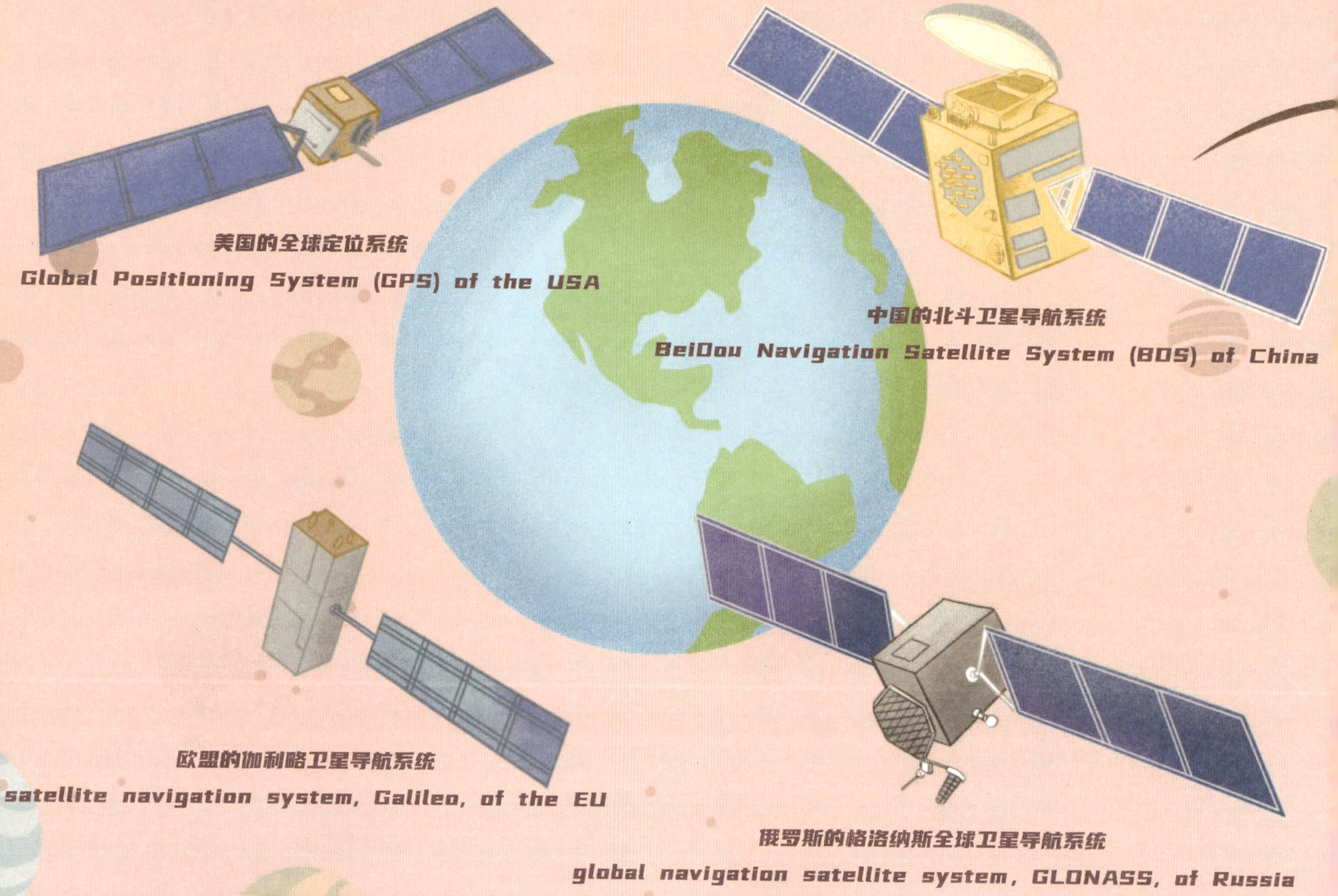

定位和导航是两个很容易被混淆的概念。定位是通过测量来确定某个人或物的地理位置。而导航则是在定位的基础上，结合实际的道路信息，提供线路规划与指引。简单来说，定位是知道自己在哪里，导航是知道自己该如何去某个地方。

Positioning and navigation are two different concepts. Positioning is to locate a person or an object through measurement. Navigation is based on positioning, combines actual road information, and provides route planning and guidance. That's to say, positioning is to know where you are, and navigation is to know how to get somewhere.

目前，最为我们熟知的导航系统是美国的全球定位系统（GPS）和中国的北斗卫星导航系统（BDS），它们以人造地球卫星为基础，为我们的日常出行提供便捷的服务。迄今为止，世界上一共有 4 个全球导航系统，除了 GPS 和 BDS 这两个我们熟知的以外，还有俄罗斯的格洛纳斯和欧盟的伽利略两个全球卫星导航系统。

Now, the most familiar navigation systems are GPS of the USA and BDS of China. They are based on artificial earth satellites, and provide convenient services for our daily travel. Up to now, there are four global navigation systems in the world. Besides GPS and BDS, there are GLONASS of Russia and Galileo of the EU.

北斗卫星导航系统是中国自主研发的全球卫星导航系统，也是世界上第三个成熟的系统。

北斗卫星导航系统能广泛应用于森林防火、抗震救灾、水文监测、气象预报和交通运输等多个领域，对社会经济发展有重要影响。在国内，北斗卫星导航系统的使用率已超过其他导航系统。

BDS is a global satellite navigation system independently developed by China, and is the third mature system in the world.

BDS can be used in many fields, such as forest fire prevention, earthquake relief, hydrological monitoring, meteorological forecasting, and transportation. It plays an important role in social and economic development. In China, the usage rate of BDS is higher than that of any other navigation system.

导航系统的“心脏”——奇妙的原子钟

“HEART” OF NAVIGATION SYSTEMS—MAGIC ATOMIC CLOCK

原子钟是一种高精度的计时装置，被认为是导航系统的“心脏”。

为什么这么说呢？

导航是通过计算我们与多个卫星之间的距离来确定位置的。当信号从某个地方出发，根据它到达卫星的时间，就可以计算出信号发射地到卫星之间的距离。而信号的传播速度是确定的，所以，时间的测算越精准，我们的定位也就越准确，而原子钟就是用来测算时间的。这就体现出原子钟的重要性啦。

The atomic clock is a high-precision timing device, and is considered the "heart" of navigation systems.

Why?

Navigation locates us by calculating the distance between us and multiple satellites. When a signal starts from a place, the distance between that place and the satellite can be calculated based on the time it takes to reach the satellite. The speed of the signal doesn't change, so the more accurate the time is, the more precise the positioning will be. The atomic clock is used for time calculation. That's why it's so important.

我们平时用的钟表，大概每年会有 1 分钟的误差。而原子钟可以实现每 2000 万年才误差 1 秒，这么高的精度使它成为科学研究中常用的工具。

The clocks we commonly use have a margin of error of about 1 minute per year. But the atomic clocks' can be only 1 second per 20 million years. Such high precision makes them a common tool in scientific research.

哇，原子钟这么厉害啊！

Wow, atomic clocks are great!

北斗“黑科技”——短报文通信

BeiDou's "Black Technology"—Short Message Communicatio

在海上与家人通信的海员

Seamen communicating with their families on the sea

短报文通信是北斗导航系统独有的服务之一，它可以利用导航卫星将个人定位以短文信息的形式发送给其他人，这是其他导航系统所不具备的。

这种功能听上去和我们的手机短信、微信信息很类似，但短报文通信能够在手机没有信号的区域，如海洋、沙漠和野外等地方发挥作用，是民生保障、救灾减灾、遇险报警、野外搜救时的好助手。

Short message communication is one of the unique services of BDS. It uses navigation satellites to send personal positioning to other people in short messages. Other navigation systems cannot do that.

This sounds like our mobile phone's text messages and WeChat messages. But short message communication is useful where mobile phone signals are not available, such as on the ocean, in the desert and in the wild. It is a good helper for people's livelihood protection, disaster relief and mitigation, distress alerting, and search and rescue in the wild.

短报文通信应用场景

Application Scenarios of Short Message Communication

在沙漠中被救援的迷路旅人

Lost traveler being rescued in the desert

气象灾害受灾地区的气象监测

Meteorological monitoring in areas stricken by meteorological disasters

在山顶拍照的小科

Kyle taking pictures on the mountain top

尾声

THE END

了解了这么多关于卫星通信的知识，小科一伸懒腰，发现自己正在帐篷里躺着。他回想着刚才学到的知识，下意识地低下头，却看到自己手机里的图片已经成功发送出去了……

After learning so much about satellite communication, Kyle stretches his arms and finds himself lying in the tent. He thinks about the new knowledge he just learned, lowers his head and suddenly sees all the pictures on his phone sent out...